DREAMS
BY NO ONE'S
DAUGHTER

Dreams by No One's Daughter

Poems
by
Leslie
Ullman

UNIVERSITY OF PITTSBURGH PRESS

Published by the University of Pittsburgh Press, Pittsburgh, Pa. 15260
Copyright © 1987, Leslie Ullman
All rights reserved
Feffer and Simons, Inc., London
Manufactured in the United States of America

Library of Congress Cataloging in Publication Data

Ullman, Leslie.
Dreams by no one's daughter.

(Pitt poetry series)
I. Title. II. Series.
PS3571.L57D7   811'.54   87–40159
ISBN 0-8229-3568-6
ISBN 0-8229-5395-1 (pbk.)

The author and publisher wish to express their grateful acknowledgment to the following publications in which some of these poems first appeared: *American Poetry Review* ("The Grocery," "Loyalty," and "Porch Light"); *Chouteau Review* ("The Rapist"); *Crazyhorse* ("Flash Flood" and "Private Acts"); *Denver Quarterly* ("Election"); *Descant* ("The Move" and "Rain in the Desert"); *Fiction International* ("American Deaf Dance Company"); *The Iowa Review* ("Running"); *Little Caesar #9* ("Care"); *Poetry* ("Dawn Feeding," "My Mother Is Not Watching," and "Peace"); *Rio Grande Review* ("Domestic Wine" and "Elsewhere"); and *Three Rivers Poetry Journal* ("The Split"). "Heat" originally appeared in *The New Yorker* in 1987.

I wish to thank all the friends with whom I've exchanged poems and commentary, that nourishment which makes revision both necessary and possible. Special thanks to the following, for their attention to large portions of this manuscript: Lewis Aptekar, Sandra Blystone, Kathleen Condon, Mark Cox, Jack Myers, Roger Sauls, and Carolyne Wright.

The publication of this book is supported by grants from the National Endowment for the Arts in Washington, D.C., a Federal agency, and the Pennsylvania Council on the Arts.

To my parents,
Frederick Ullman and Ann Riegelman Ullman

CONTENTS

1

HARD CIDER

Even to those who are dying, the season
shows its hand, filling the ditches
with jewels: mica fish and emerald mallards.
Draft horses prance in their filigreed
traces, heady with sun and a premonition
of frost. They barely touch the earth

as the farmers themselves spring from the ground,
in their prime, their wooden clogs
caked with sweet mud. Everything they touch
turns to sheaves, loaves, luminous
preserves; the scent of cooking strains
at walls and beams that surround

young wives. And everywhere trees, having
borne the brunt of summer,
rise stately as half-clothed women lifting
baskets to their heads. They have waited
in greenery and silence, suddenly
to cradle perfect apples.

Even to those who are dying, this land looks
as it would from the air, or to a Sunday painter
dozing on a hill—a quilt of gardens and threading streams,
hills in waves, green squares, russets, gleaming
pitchfork, the painted noontime jug. No smell of old sweat
lingering in homespun. No hard words with the wife.

No palm across the cheek, tears, thin gruels
in the early dusk that gathers itself up north.
Even to those who are dying, the last of the hummingbirds
is a bright leaf riding the wind, and the hawk
sharing its patch of sky for a time
too plump, too brightly feathered, to kill.

3

THE ORIGIN OF TEARS

You're about to speak
and they take you
by surprise, little natives
beating drums in your throat.
A music the body listens to.
The push the lump from its
familiar cave, and your chest
aches with loosened rock.

Now your face melts, a child face,
boneless again in a landscape that blurs
to the salt water the world
once was, and your body cracks
into islands and fish and
bottomless space that somehow

does not fly apart.
The bird inside you screams.

You don't make a sound. Grief,
dreaming among the fallen trees,
answers, suddenly light on his feet—

he seizes your dry
pod of a heart, summons
voice after voice you never use,
and now you are dancing, unable
to return to your country, hostage
until he has finished dance after dance

with you, over white-hot words
you couldn't say when you first
learned to talk.

PRIVATE ACTS

My father promised,
as he shut my door, night
was the sun's eye
blinking. I promised

I wouldn't chew paper
again, or leave the damp wads
like amulets under the bed.
I shut my eyes. The guests

raised their drinks and told stories
downstairs, laughing in their
bracelets. Their rings of smoke.
Their strange breath bloomed

with attention. I opened my eyes
but the paisley sofa rose
anyway, a copper wave that filled
and kept filling my eye's black room.

I crept to the stairs where light
floated up, and sometimes
a string of words I wanted
to wear for the night. . . .

He tucked me in again.
He promised me dark
as a pair of arms, rocking
water, a blanket my size. . . .

The paper tasted salty,
the taste of my first lie.
Then I crept into the waves
of scented furs on the bed no one

made my parents sleep in—
no, I slept all night
in the bed where I
belonged, while turquoise threads

branched like bits of sky
through my mother's water-colored
gown, and the gray morning
leaked into all the windows at once.

PORCH LIGHT

He has begun the war like a promising story,
the end of his boyhood;
last night the first plane he ever saw
hovered, surprisingly small
over this shrill city

where no one speaks English.
His father often spoke of seeing the world.
Once he said, "I'm leaving," and his mother
put her face in her hands, drained
of what she was saying

and the silence softened between them for days.
He halts among the crushed tiles,
the partial shade of walls that glowed
all night under fire. On the other side of the ocean
his parents doze in their wicker chairs.

The butter warms to a glaze on their plates,
to memory; their street turns golden.
Later he'll see this street
he scarcely sees: the ash that settles
in the sun, over balconies, the bedclothes

collapsing and filling with wind.
The war, unsure of itself, keeps moving
aside. Dusk has arrived on the other side
of the ocean. Later in the dark, he
slouches, and whistles softly on the bottom stair.

MY MOTHER IS NOT WATCHING

from the door as I start my first
walk to school. I am not afraid

though this crisp eyelet
dress feels like someone else's skin

and these houses
tall faces turning

away. This morning
my mother gets to stay

where she chooses, raising
one shoulder, cradling the phone

so her hands are free to coat each
nail to a shield over each

pale finger. Smoke from her cigarette
curls across the table like the breath

of a visitor, the glamorous
woman she secretly loves.

In this dress I'm her dream
and no one's daughter.

School is a story whose ending
she tells me she doesn't know.

Now she opens the paper to follow
a war far away, while I march

into autumn, beneath the fences
and high windows which in time

I won't see, just
the blackboard worn thin

with words that vanish
each night. I will find my way

through their sounds, a song
unwinding, and one day

I will open a book and not
notice I'm reading.

FLASH FLOOD

My parents call to say, *Are you*
all right, we can't sleep, you
shouldn't be alone. Again
I tell them I live on a hill,

that it's only the rain
beating like robbers at the window.
They tell me, *We've never liked*
you living alone, when

are you coming home,
and now I remember all
the beaux who borrowed money,
the bath I once left running,

the ceiling cracking
under where I should have been,
the tantrums, the anniversaries,
the notes of thanks.

The president rises on the news
from another public meal
where food lies on his plate
like an abandoned village, prodded

and intact. I rise to fix a sandwich.
I walk softly for the neighbors
downstairs, while somewhere at sea
in a wallet warmed by a sailor's hip

a child stares boldly from his
mother's lap as though the camera
were an eye just opening
the world to him.

THE MOVE

Overnight your street has grown blank with doors.
With sunlight slammed into glass.
Mornings, other summers, the screens hummed.

Cricket sounds razored through sunrise,
shade and dripping leaves.
Your bare feet left shadows in the wet grass.

This morning fine cracks have surfaced
in the pavement and the corners of your eyes
though your neighbors, as usual, quickly

finish their toast as they head for their cars,
flag down the bus, smoothe their hair
which shows no gray. They wave to one another

over your lawn as it bakes to sand
again. After you leave, it will
finish a journey of its own.

*

In the dream you decide to give away books
and the antique gown

that fits so well, waiting for its occasion
because you are in a house you remember.

A house lit by water outside.
The floors and empty shelves

gleam like sculpture.

*

You take the paintings down—
the grillworks of ink, petals
and greens crowding their frames.
You hand yourself plate after plate
filling the walls with white,
the cupboards with air.

On long days like this, your
parents' house melted to garden,
rainfall, a bank of cut grass.
You read for the last time
the letters you've read
too quickly to throw away.
By noon your roof has burned
thin, and the fine grit
that blows all day has found
its way into the floorboards,
the jade plants, your hands.

The lake closed around you.
That scent of other lives.
You rode waves in the sun
till they called you inside.
Your body still swayed at dinner.
You wrap the silver, fold the towels.

✿

This morning you wake moving
your legs, your breath
going wrong against the ribs.
Today you will turn from this house

and you do. *At first they held you*
over the shallows while you moved
one arm, then the other.
The reeds waved and waved
underwater, that other wind

and your body dangled
out of their way
like a jacket blown from the boat.
Keep breathing, they said.
Look away from the shore.

CARE

She dressed me in white
and sent me to the garden
after breakfast; *for years*
I believe it another
room in which I mustn't move.
She kept still in the next
room, while another child's flesh
gathered, then grew away from bone.
All day the sun sets fires
in the leaves. I am the princess
whose white skin opens
and heals on a bed of stones.
Sometimes she sat late
by my bed and spoke
of cabbages that turned into
swans. Into men.
And sometimes she didn't call me
before the last tree
disappeared. For years
her hand lingered on the lamp.

PLACES I CIRCLE BACK TO

The first time no one listened
becomes that home I seek
again and again when I
speak, thinking each time
my voice carries—
it vanishes in others'
visible breath. I haven't found
a room I can fill.

Outside, plants grow and shed leaves
where they find themselves, and the horses
stamp at flies without a trace
of anger. Sometimes I vanish
comfortably under the sun
and undivided sky

while puddles shrink
invisibly after days of rain
leaving, instead of dust, a mud
that holds everything in place—
this is how the ground gives up
the moisture that has come
and come to it beyond
what it can drink. A blessed

tiredness. As sometimes when I'm reading
and the words pull themselves into a story—
into a person more right than wrong
in a recognizable dilemma—
someone not blurred by decisions
or divided into faulty halves

but leaning into
her fate, one long dance,
as into a day of work. As into
days of work we seek
and do and seek respite from, to
tell ourselves we are really here.

II

PEACE

Keep your voice down, my husband
hissed this morning across his plate,
then knotted his tie
to a fist that would hold
all day. Wedged in our thin
walls against the silence of neighbors
we haven't met, I folded
my napkin, shoved the last word
back in my throat
and later jogged extra laps
as though my feet could make
some mark on firm ground,
could make everything clear.
I remove my damp
sweatclothes, shivering now
in the best boutique I can find.
An older woman shrugs out of a fur
soft as fog and gathers up jade, silver,
apple-green silks, all hushed
and viciously expensive.

She wraps herself in a gown
the color of doves, a shadow body
that follows no husband. I'm sure their house
holds a room where she dreams,
sends letters, while someone downstairs
seasons the greens and filets
and a reasonable hunger warms her like firelight.
If her children should quarrel
on the darkening lawn she drifts outside
to soothe each with a story, her voice adding
girth to itself like the wine,
open, breathing by his plate.

19

I want to ask for my size
in a gown like hers. I want to fill
a gown with breasts like hers, and move
through our rooms like a boat
through any water. I finger aqua silk
made for real hips and shoulders
I, too, could have after twenty seasons—

it turns a whole room blue
where I enter myself as I dress,
where my garments turn overhead light
back on itself like fine paintings.
Downstairs he slices meat striped with fat
and pink flesh, while I finger each
pearl on the choker he gave me when money
was tight. The blue folds drift
over my body, that house
filled with rooms left by daughters
and sons, that house given over
to pale silk and stone, its silence
my secret, my eyes raised
to meet hers in the triple mirror.

THE RAPIST

You do not know how long
he sat by the bed
moving the hidden
parts of your body.
to another mattress
in his head.
You never saw his face.
Later, police found
bits of the kitchen window
tracked with damp soil
through every room.

❀

Your first lover was
a large man, soft
from years of longing
for extraordinary women,
and had small hands.
His skin burned easily in the sun.
That first night,
pleased and desperate,
he licked parts of your body
you'd never seen,
then shuddered, settled,
and drifted in your arms.

You were too pleased to sleep.
You arranged yourself carefully
over your sore parts.
All night his eyes moved

21

under soft, blue lids
as though seeking
the other women he'd leave
asleep. Awake, you would
ease him into daylight.

❁

Inside your body, the doctor
found hairs
with tweezers
and a pinpoint
of light. "The police,"
he said, "will keep them
for evidence."

❁

You keep telling yourself he
was not a large man.
His body in each hot bath
loosens from yours like paint.
Night after night your breasts
are weightless in the water, neither
plants nor animals, are laced
with stubborn blue veins.
All night your eyes move under
dark lids, as though seeking
a familiar woman inside yourself.

AMERICAN DEAF DANCE COMPANY

They mark stress
as the sting of landing,
swift kiss, another
leap apart.
I lean in my seat
missing you. My knees
crack. Our old dispute
loosens its whims,
the backward curl of our words
on themselves,
the silence we kept
as we left for a movie.

Walking home, we held
the plot like ice
in our mouths while streetlight
sent our shadows ahead—
we never followed them, children
in the pale street,
we never walked
barefoot through the house. . . .

Loose cotton sweeps
their skin, their breath
the only other sound.
Their eyes never
leave the space
they weave, leaving
the ground, and I
clap my hands high
so they'll see—
she falls again
into his sure arms.

THE GROCERY

She wants to arrange
these melons and limes,
these oranges, these
pears on a frosted plate
but her hands wait. The day
burns. The fresh trout
would shrivel in lemon
and salt; she has lost her
luck in the kitchen.

Even parsley
curls her tongue.
She has lost the man
who's gone with the friend
in herself, and that's
the ache, *her* arms, the old
taste for talk, and these black
plums suddenly in season.

The aisles fill
with strangers who
move among these offerings
with the ease of the loved.
Their fingers disappear into
the freshly sprayed greens.
Later, their arms will interrupt
the light over their plates
to pass the wine, to take
some space in the room
while she, turning

invisible as she once
wanted to be, will feed herself
without thought—the last child hiding
in the neighbors' hedge as it
vanished every night,
bearing her away from the gold windows.

THE SPLIT

This evening I carry myself
gently. Rain softens
our lawn. In another woman's
house, your sorrow lifts off

and leaves you amazed;
her hand on your cheek
is more real than any secret
flesh. This rain sounds

like women whispering,
and I want to tell you,
I can feel them touch
my face. You feel her touch

let you out of your body
as though a child
of your own stood nearby.
A sad woman with fine

luminous hair,
she sees herself
as a rumor, and now you must
tell her not to leave you.

RUNNING

Lately my neighbor wheezes
pounding dough, her forearms
glazed with sweat and flour.
"At your age," my mother
writes, "I wanted babies
and got pregnant
each time one of you
learned to walk."
I circle the block again
and again, until I run
outside my body.
This time last year
my husband stopped
speaking of the other woman
who slept poorly inside him.

She promised in another town
to give him up. All night she
tossed and tried to speak
until he spoke of his
father, who drank himself
into the cracked
well of his voice
and never touched bottom.
She made him wake sweating
and brooding in the closed
room of his departure
while I ran myself past
my neighbor's lawn and plump
loaves settling in their heat
to an early shape of myself.

ii

I'd forgotten the apartment
that stretched like a tunnel,
shapeless and dark
the way my good dress hung
too large, a formal
body outside my body.
The other men drifted
alike behind their drinks
while he stood in one place
and spoke to me of *The Moviegoer*
which spoke, he said, to his very soul.

Sometimes I run in Louisiana
where I've never been,
where the hero saw an egret gather
itself over swamp mist
and settle in a single oak
that rose to meet it.
Later he married his cousin
whose agile mind wandered,
glittering at the family table.
The dense mahogany.
The black butler
wheezed as he passed the beans.
She couldn't sleep, she
said, without pills.
Sometimes she slept for two days.
She promised she could
be like anyone, if he
would tell her each morning
how to pass that day.

28

That night, my skin
held me like liquid glass.
I wanted to slip
my hand beneath his elbow,
to dance, to see the other women
naked inside their clothes.

iii

Every morning I run
through pollen, late summer
haze, and rain. My husband
is an illness I had
in another country.

The day he left
again and again he said
it wasn't your fault.
I circle the block, pump
and sweat until I run
outside my body.
My ribs ache.
He brushed his hands
gently over them.

Inside my running
I write to him, breaking
the silence we keep
for his new wife:
I saw the sun disappear
into mist as it reached
the horizon. And an egret
airborne, circling all
this time.

The morning bus gathers
husbands and children
and leaves for a moment
a soft rope of exhaust.
I draw breath over breath
as the children

must breathe in their sleep.
My neighbor waves
from her doorway, follows my
easy stride: "Your waist,"
she says wistfully,
"fits the dress I wore as a bride."

LOYALTY

Our eyes meet over other
couples' shoulders, and another

love song launches its vows.
His body lists

in my direction but not,
I assure myself,

without grace. I offer my
ringless hand: "Shall we dance?"

On his waist my hand meets
the roll of flesh, the wife

he left who let her body go.
I remind myself there's no such thing

as a badly made man.
"Your eyes . . ." he says

and my glasses slip into their silk
purse. His chin settles into

my neck. "The pearls," I
say, "were a gift

from the man I didn't marry."
Tall, dark, and riddled

with beauty, he spent my ardor
to please, pressing any

knees under glass
tables. This one

breathes in my ear
with the two-step. I

rise to my toes to
follow on air. Oh, I learned

to stay calm on that phone
while a stranger breathed hard

words of love. Now my life
is about to change.

He tells me his mistress,
all legs and caramel

skin, just left for the coast.
We dance, we drink, we doze

on each other's shoulders.
We peer at the stars

which stay in their dark
and gather ourselves toward

morning, the hard sun,
the rough ride out of our clothes.

THE COALS THE DAY HAS COME TO

In the novel I've brought, the heroine
who resembles me suddenly
is all cheekbone and wild hair. Introspection
etches her thin as a spinster, even as
the waitress sets down my cup. Caffeine
and air. I hear the man at the next table

closing his paper. And the woman
he's waited for loosening her hair,
letting, she murmurs, the goddess
surface at last. I imagine him
tilted over his cup, drinking her in
and their story forming itself before they speak—
the malaise that swelled in his heart
overnight, the brandy finished at dawn,
the letter she wrote over and over
and left with the night clerk.

I order another. The sky has darkened
out there over traffic and large firms
and hundreds of empty rooms throb
with light. The workers have stepped
out of their thick-soled shoes, out of their
sleep, and the legs of my waitress gleam
in transparent black stockings.
I order another. The woman at the next table
lifts her hand to catch the light
as though she has never seen it before, that hand
which she'll slip into a glove the color
of evening, that hand
with its five ruby nails and a diamond.

DOMESTIC WINE

My friends are quitting cigarettes,
being quoted on the news,
dividing their property,
and watching every foreign film.
Each plans to move to some city
that sprawls over water,
a life alone.
Each is the hero

in a story that begins,
"I've never told this to anyone,"
my friends at dawn in their swift
canvas shoes and their remnants
of breath, my friends packing
weathered valises, my friends
in polished skin and turquoise.
Their good bones surface

like carvings over the tables
they've stripped and waxed
and waxed again. Even the air
takes shape between their hands
as each, like a bandit, plans
to slip from the crowd.
Part of me takes me out, drinks
too much tonight, and murmurs
I'm moving south.

Lately we can feel lines
sprouting from our eyes,
the corners of our mouth.
She raises our glass,

you'll look marvelous in ten years,
then heads for the buffet. She
eats anything, while I open my mouth
to listen: one vows not

to marry again; one sleeps
without pills now, pretending
herself held by someone she's
never met; another began to fall
carefully in love last night
over a bottle of good cabernet.
One by one they tell me,
"The worst is over. Now
I know my way."

ELECTION

Today I'd like to think the sky
is the limit. And this yellow kitchen
something more than air between coals
and cold gasses, winds, urgent voices. . . .
The trees dive overnight into gold.
Again they've done it as a gift to me

at the window, to you nosing disgruntled
into traffic. The weather
will take it all back as another
election, another carnival ship
cracks the horizon with flags
and barrels of beer, new friends

who look like old friends, arguments
juxtaposed and clicking into place,
picked bone, old socket, death
by air, death by flame,
this morning's paper rolled fat

with warnings. I open it, then find
myself counting potatoes at the sink,
parting one tight hide at a time
from one tough heart. I watch leaves
outside cut loose and swirl
away from trampled paths.

I find my hands at the small
of my back, giving comfort
to that place where my body keeps
its bargain, keeps standing,
as huge vans on their winter tires
gather speed past the house.

SOLSTICE

Yesterday my neighbor stepped outdoors
in a robe silly with roses.
She's new to these mornings. To the hills
packed in clouds. Gray fingers skim
the gardens. Animals sleep underground.
I stood at my window in a long
sleep of my own, while my hand brushed
the spoon and blue cup. She gathered
her paper rolled into itself like mine
from a lawn closed like mine.
The roses glared below her face.

Then last night the scent of peaches,
if that's possible, drifted
from her house, with piñion
she may kindle tonight,
piñon that grew into whole summers
in high, thinned air. My legs
quickened with the pleasure of
climbing and coming home.
I woke remembering her skin,
veined and pale in that first light

as changeable and clear as rain.
Ground coffee breathed
from her kitchen, and she was
smiling to herself, as though the earth
might flare green at any moment,
its blossoms bowing at her door.

This morning I watch the sky lift itself
over our windows. The trees open their
slow limbs. When she steps outside
the roses have softened below
her face, ivory against thick hair
but furrowed in the candid sun.
Tonight I'll open wine I've been saving.

DREAMS BY NO ONE'S DAUGHTER

I

Daylight. For everyone but me. *Nap*
is a night word, a shade they pull
every afternoon against sunlight and speckled leaves
which come to my room anyway
with the telephone ringing downstairs, the boy
across the street, in a tree, shouting
to his friends, and cars' tires
heavy on gravel. *I'm not tired.*

My hand suddenly is a friend
opening and closing like a secret plan
on its silent hinges. It is not
fat anymore like my brother's,
this hand growing up by itself,
this hand hugged in skin the color of sand,
this hand that blooms from my wrist
in a world of chance. *Hand.* Mine.

Something fills me now, like water
but not water—a feeling
in my head. *Idea* of hand.
I float over the bed while everyone
thinks I'm asleep
and my hand begins to remember growing
in the dark, finger by finger,
then the dream, the swim, parting
the dark to touch skin, face, cup, flame,
my mother's sharp red nails,
my grandmother's creased map of veins
and her mother's ring
so green it turns my eyes into stones.

41

II

Emerald. It anchored my grandmother's hand
at the head of the table. At her touch
the brass bell sang, the consommé arrived
and disappeared in its scallopped tureen, and glass plates
floated on the maid's hands like mirrors.
It leaked sea light through the fingers
of her other hand, clasped over it in dimmed Carnegie Hall
while music swelled toward the busy ceiling.
It flashed under chandeliers at receptions and
foreign hotels, splitting the air into rainbow
and ice like the stars, the bubbles in
crystal, laughter in the night.
Now it smolders over my mother's thickening knuckle
in the house where I grew up, all those long afternoons
of trump cards and tea. Someone's gardener
burning the last of the leaves. It slips in and out
of its velvet box. It slips in and out of Sundays.
It waits under her black gloves at funerals.

III

That was another life, when it found its way
to my third finger, right hand.
I wore black silk
and painted my nails coral.
I took my coffee
without honey, sherry at five,
and brandy from a slender glass before bed.
I did not live between
two fields, one cotton and one alfalfa.
The sky did not fill the days with
silence and depths of blue
while the skin loosened slowly about my knuckles.
I moved among symphonies, dinners
served by strangers, and buildings
that pressed like thieves against each other's windows.
I did not measure oats every morning
for two chestnut geldings.
I did not watch the sun vanish
every night in its nest of coals.
I locked my doors. I left on all the lamps
against the soft, mysterious night.
I did not tell story after story to
myself, like a child believed to be asleep.

LIVING NEAR THE PLAZA OF THIEVES

Three floors up, I fall
asleep to footsteps rising.
Somebody's door lets out
syllables whose music thickens the air.
All night traffic breathes
water, sound through a shell, and I
follow the Sexta, the Quinta,
the Avenida del Rio, where language
flows past me in the careless
currency of speech.

The words, the whole country
I'm chipped from, dissolve.
I leave nothing behind as I follow
the dusty child who sometimes
follows me—maybe he sleeps
under a bridge, maybe the smell
of cooking draws him
closer to guarded doors.

The man who watches this building
blows his whistle, barely
nudging the air. He reminds me
to look for myself where
I am—next door to a woman
whose husband I've never seen
and a plump bachelor who keeps
rattling his keys. A radio
fills suddenly with tambourines

and I am wrapped around my purse,
staring into the dark
that is not a window. The real
window takes shape against a streak
of dawn as the watchman mutters sharp
words, pebbles flung into the street.
All night I try to finish
a sentence in another language,
the silence I break in letters home.

IN THE ANDES

The diesel coughs
as I lose my breath to
stunning air. Tracks climb
into the past ahead—now we
stop. Night. Mountain walls.
The other travelers sing,

tell stories, they fill the train
with phrases they've carried into
lobbies, tearooms, offers
for silver and wool.
I listen for a country
in their voices. I hear instead

a sigh rising from the dusk
all around—it's the river
fanning itself against dark
rock, the one clear
way out, a gleaming scar
how many years deep?

Clouds drift
close enough to mix
with my breath. The train
has gone. The train
never was. Rain
lulls me against this slope
as though sky had been water all along.

WIND

Already the morning is thick with earth
trying to be air. And I'm trying at my desk
to wrap myself in another room, where a single lamp
throws anchor into dawn, sunset, the dizzying
pull of the sun. Or a steady rain outside fastens
everything down. Any book I open takes root and spreads
into thought, page after page pressed beneath glass.

A few desert wrens looking for thrown seed
drop out of the sky, starting the world over.
The morning turns even thicker, less real.
It turns to a kind of water, and I think of things I
value only because I've lost them—gray glove,
another pen, an amber stone loosened from its setting
while at my desk, my car surrounds me at breakneck speed

as it will soon enough, between an explosion of
skyscrapers on my left and the Rio Grande dozing
on my right, cloudy with silt and dismantled winters.
Sprawled against the other side, Mexico wakes in its breath
of slow-cooking beans, cilantro, salsa, mesquite,
wakes in its pastel huts that bleed into the glare—
I would lean against the peeling paint of a doorway
and watch the street fill with children in bright clothes,
but I'm rushing through the afternoon to where I sit now.

This wide valley. Water creeps from the border
to feed the red chilies, waves of red chilies, their scent
the only color left in the room. A worker guides his bike
along the dirt road outside. I lean into the dust of his world
with my windows cracked open, sweat drying on my forehead,
my hands loosening on the wheel.

POISON

I came in hot, shedding clothes,
my mind rinsing off grit and hours of wind
when a hissing wove itself
through the air. Not the usual
cricket, not an indoor sound at all,
this noise slipped from a story
I began to remember—dried bones. Wind
through stripped branches. The sun probing
layers of dust and driving everything alive
towards shelter. Then I saw the coil
of sand and diamond ash on the bathmat
where, stepping into water,
I would have met the blind rush
to a doctor, my body not mine at all.
I came back with a hoe
but it had vanished, leaving my house
filled with lies. Long muscle. The trash
grown fragrant with chicken bone and apple peel.
Its shadow children
curled among the laundered sheets.

Tonight these walls close in
the way the sound of my own voice did once
in a taxi in a dream, as the driver
kept speeding down the wrong
dark street. Tonight the freezer
and water heater mumble in another room
like visitors, and I don't live anymore with the me
who grabbed for the hoe,

ready to split another life into small
talk about living with the desert.
I sit up late. I put my feet
on the desk, and watch the moon
so full my window can't hold it
floating, a miner's lamp in a cave
while the room behind me fills with
teeth. Hot breath. Old quarrels. Shadows
meeting beyond the reading lamp's reach.

RAIN IN THE DESERT

It leaves this city suddenly
porous, all windows
thrown open. Whatever grows

out there in the sand comes in
close, exhaling its own scent
like the gray horse that once

detached himself at dusk
from the dark end of a pasture.
I'd thought he was a shed

or space between pines
and I want to laugh
again, this time

having been right all day—
how my temples closed over
grievances, fat around the heart,

then flared—I wanted sudden
stones across old water,
a vein of pure logic, someone

to grab my hands.
Now the sun offers the last
of itself, a bruised light

where the horizon has pulled
the sky apart. And the beaten
streets, dark rivers, shine

as though through tears.

FORESTS

We bring a memory she leans toward
like a pale shoot. We bring
the smell of last night's rain.
We bring new husbands and wives
whose names she cannot lift from
the dark magnet of her thoughts pulling
her face inward, leaving patches of shadow.

She hardly speaks now of the last
house in the row where a forest bloomed
from her lawn into another home.
She walked us one by one
through its green rooms, naming
what belonged in them—
lupine, larkspur, nuthatch, wren. . . .

And when I wandered in alone
one day, too small to connect
so many hallways. I held those names
like tablets under my tongue. Her voice
filled the woods and led me past signs
I could read: Trillium, that blaze
of white we found only once.
Cedar, tree split by wind. Violets
scattered in the shape of a hand.

Today is her birthday. Her chair on wheels
is a pallet in a clearing, and the weather
in the hallway perilous with light.
We've brought hothouse mums, an orchid,
and roses rooted now in water.
We've brought a first great-granddaughter

who has just discovered a patch
of sunlight on the floor—
how it shivers with leaf
shadows—she hoists herself
on miraculous legs and walks
into it, out, and in again, toward
all the hands this air reaches out to her.

HEAT

When we first arrived, nothing
seemed to be growing, the brown
a kind of final color. Even cottonwoods
in their dust and tortured bark were another
form of rock. I flinched from the sky, trying
to find room, that summer of cracked skin

where the river used to be. Dried grass,
the real frontier, blew white across my brow,
and all through the drought's expected
deprivations, we spoke less and less.
I rubbed my dry face until I drew blood.

One day something alive at my feet sent up
a pale green smell. Aged water and sun.
Quail suddenly gathered themselves
from the sand, thrumming with purpose,
and then I noticed miniature leaves
close to the ground making secret cover.
"Sage," you told me later, when I opened my palm.

Sunset began to pick out the dunes
earlier each afternoon. They bloomed peach,
rose, before their shadows spread over the valley
into one element. Water. It stroked our house until
the windows filled with ordinary light.
And every evening the neighbor's gentle horses
paced their corral, in the darkness, waiting
for their hay. Every evening they were
hungry. Then they were happy.

FORTY

The pomegranates in my yard are raucous
and sun-stroked, leathery with
summer, hard to break into.

The seeds inside, who knows
how many, still shore up
juices in the dark, though each globe

had been bold and red as an apple since May.
Now the sun leans away from the garden
keeping its other promises.

September, the nights trail
cooling air, and the unfinished seeds
nip the tongue.

October. They taste
pale pink, lingering.
First frost, and they fill the mouth

with sunlight and wine,
wave after wave of sunlight and wine . . .
for so long the tree just bore bright flowers.

DAWN FEEDING

Darkness has feathered all night
downward into drifts. Vague bits of
dream. Discarded socks and shirt.
My feet sink in and track it
outside, where what's near
still recedes—woodpile, corral, the bay
mare's heavy head nodding
between the rails—I'm not
ready to open my other eyes.

The hungry horses loom like ships,
restless and dark against the sky.
One pokes a blunt nose out of the night,
into my hand, and a dream I had before waking
takes shape again—a familiar child,
my brother's new daughter left to my care
like the life-sized doll I was given
one birthday, a time I was really part horse.
She was too expensive to be taken from her box.
"When you're older," they promised. Nearly
forty now, I kept forgetting to carry crackers
and milk to the hidden room where this child
drifted in her crib. Little by little she stopped
inventing words. Her warm cheeks
cooled to wax. I never even thought
to pick her up, my arms weren't real
as they weren't in the days when I
flourished my silk scarf of a tail.
When I munched what I was fed. When I tossed
my head and slept hard. Daylight

abruptly has flooded this yard.
My neglect, my night track, does not
burn off, but the horses turn to me
anyway, the bringer of buckets and hay.
All night they held some shape
of me in their heads like a dream —
a snip of red, perhaps, a weightless thing
drifting in and out of their view.
Now they dip their heads in the circle
of my arms. Their jaws closing over
the charged and magical grains are engines
churning up steam that would startle
their vast bodies away, even now,
if I raised a hand to them suddenly.

PITT POETRY SERIES
Ed Ochester, General Editor

Tom Lowenstein, tr., *Eskimo Poems from Canada and Greenland*
Archibald MacLeish, *The Great American Fourth of July Parade*
Peter Meinke, *Night Watch on the Chesapeake*
Peter Meinke, *Trying to Surprise God*
Judith Minty, *In the Presence of Mothers*
Carol Muske, *Camouflage*
Carol Muske, *Wyndmere*
Leonard Nathan, *Carrying On: New & Selected Poems*
Leonard Nathan, *Dear Blood*
Leonard Nathan, *Holding Patterns*
Kathleen Norris, *The Middle of the World*
Sharon Olds, *Satan Says*
Alicia Ostriker, *The Imaginary Lover*
Greg Pape, *Black Branches*
Greg Pape, *Border Crossings*
James Reiss, *Express*
William Pitt Root, *Faultdancing*
Liz Rosenberg, *The Fire Music*
Dennis Scott, *Uncle Time*
Herbert Scott, *Groceries*
Richard Shelton, *Of All the Dirty Words*
Richard Shelton, *Selected Poems, 1969-1981*
Richard Shelton, *You Can't Have Everything*
Arthur Smith, *Elegy on Independence Day*
Gary Soto, *Black Hair*
Gary Soto, *The Elements of San Joaquin*
Gary Soto, *The Tale of Sunlight*
Gary Soto, *Where Sparrows Work Hard*
Tomas Tranströmer, *Windows & Stones: Selected Poems*
Chase Twichell, *Northern Spy*
Chase Twichell, *The Odds*
Leslie Ullman, *Dreams by No One's Daughter*
Constance Urdang, *The Lone Woman and Others*
Constance Urdang, *Only the World*
Ronald Wallace, *People and Dog in the Sun*
Ronald Wallace, *Tunes for Bears to Dance To*
Cary Waterman, *The Salamander Migration and Other Poems*
Bruce Weigl, *A Romance*
Robley Wilson, Jr., *Kingdoms of the Ordinary*
David Wojahn, *Glassworks*
David P. Young, *The Names of a Hare in English*
Paul Zimmer, *Family Reunion: Selected and New Poems*